Opening In The Sky

Armand Garnet Ruffo

Theytus Books Ltd.
Penticton, B.C.
Canada

All poems. Copyright 1994: Armand Garnet Ruffo.

First Edition

All rights reserved. No part of this book covered by the copyright herein may be reproduced or transmitted in any form by any means graphic, electronic or mechanical, including photocopying, recording or any information storage, retrieval and transmission systems, without permission in writing from the publisher, except by a reviewer who may quote brief passages in a review.

Theytus Books Ltd. 257 Brunswick St., Penticton, B.C., V2A 5P9.
Book design and typesetting: Marlena Dolan.
Art work: Leo Yerxa. Courtesy of the artist.

Printed and bound in Canada.

Canadian Cataloguing in Publication Data

Ruffo, Armand Garnet, 1955-
Opening In The Sky

Poems
ISBN 0-919441-55-6

I. Indians of North America--Canada--Poetry. 1. Title.
PS8585.U33063 1994   C811'.54   C94-910496-56
PR9199.3.R83063 1994

The publisher acknowledges the support of the Canada Council, Department of Communications and the Cultural Services Branch of the Province of British Columbia in the publication of this book.

Acknowledgements: Some of the poems (in one form or another) first appeared in the following publications:

Northward Journal, Anthos, The Blue Cloud Quarterly (USA), The Magazine to Re-Establish the Trickster, Passages, SAIL (Studies in American Indian Literatures, USA) Contemporary Native Literature: Seventh Generation, Mr. Cogito (USA), The New Quarterly, Dandelion, Gatherings, Native Literature in Canada, Poetry WLU, Wayzgoose, Environment in Perspective, Contemporary Verse 2, Callaloo (USA), absinthe, Voices from Home.

Some of the poems were broadcast on CBC Radio's *Open House* and read at A Space Art Gallery, Toronto; the Banff Centre for the Arts; the Ottawa Valley Book Festival du Livre des Outaouais, the Museum of Civilization, Hull; the University of Oklahoma, *Returning the Gift* Native writer's conference, Norman, Oklahoma.

A warm thank you to all those who gave me much needed support and encouragement, in particular to the late Adele Wiseman who invited me to the Banff Centre of the Arts where some of these poems were written, and to Jeannette Armstrong who helped me select and organize the poems for this collection. Meeg-wetch to all.

For family and all those still coming to terms with what happened.

Contents:

9	Upon Returning
10	Paleo Song
11	Bear Death
12	When It Came
13	Sunday Change
14	Mandate (For the angry young warrior)
15	8 o'clock Monday Morning
16	Night Vision
17	Descent
18	The Storm
19	Voice
20	Passage
23	Theatre Indigenous
24	Sahquakegick
25	Poem For Duncan Campbell Scott
26	Man To Man
27	Christoforo Colombo Claims America, 1492
29	Settlers
30	The Man
31	Claim
32	The Other Side Of The Looking Glass
33	Creating A Country
35	What Kind Of Man
36	Almighty Voice
37	Crow Children
41	Let The Oppressed Sing
43	You, Your Father, The Indians and Life
44	On Lake Titicaca
45	Tunisia After The Rain
46	Some
48	January City
49	No Questions Asked
50	Sociable
51	On The Street
52	Shine
53	Untitled
54	Public Education
55	Pale Face
56	Hospital Visit

61	December
63	Conversation
65	Demand
66	Trickster
67	Emotion
68	Poetry
69	Chant For Mother And Child
70	Influences
72	Hunter
73	Surely Not Warriors
74	10 Park Poems
77	Long Distance
81	Old Story
82	With These Hands
83	Home
84	Their Own
85	Once We Went Fishing
86	Protect The Island
87	The Trout Become The Day Later That Evening
88	Kebsquasheshing
89	Poem For Esher
90	After The Hunt
91	Rock Bottom Lake
92	The Season

Upon Returning

In this everything I disclose
is known beforehand.
There are no fresh tracks
to follow here, no sign
leading to a new direction.

On the front street my footprints,
a procession
of solemn signatures,
lie like dried flowers.

If you stare hard enough
into the concrete
you will agree. If this is unbearable
you can watch me methodically
on my hands
and knees.

To celebrate the occasion
of returning
I am collecting
as many as I can
just to try them on
for size
merely to see how much
I've grown
(changed with the walk).

Paleo Song

Sing under a face of moon,
dawn of story,
eye of time,
starry arrows, hunter
            and bear child,
skin of voice drumming east.

paleozoic - paleocene - gene,
paleo
map of the heart,
       ocher and stone,
     shaft of
           bone.

Sing your gift
          straight and true,
and you do,
simple and strong
as tongues
that have risen on fin
descended on wing
born of earth
and breath
as the song goes.

Bear Death

Familiar with bear death
I have seen him served as an offering
hot on a plate, supper for the successful.
Penis bone scraped clean
and drying in the sun. Caged
corpse braided in tassels
and bells, lying like a rug.
Head stuffed.

Squat on a log dreaming slick ants
thick as people or thick people slick
as ants was the first time he was shot.
Right between the eyes.
It was raining a smell
of earth and water.

If I say today he's bent and lumbering
over your city streets   believe me.
The faces he sees are smudged against glass.
Enticed by flesh's soft currency, he is expected
to eat heartily, lick his lips
and join the crowd.
He tries to keep his head, take only
the choice bits, give
only the odd unfamiliar
    growl.

When It Came

When it came over
   the radio
      someone
         was hacking
            the beaks
off birds   it came to me
somewhere   someone
(that same person) was caught
  in his own cage
     was killing
        to get out
holding on
to the bloodied pieces
hoping for flight.

Sunday Change

I toss yesterday's clothes aside
empty they are formless rags
which no one has worn but me.
spring grows
and the bear crawls from hibernation.
somewhere he is not thinking
of what he has left behind.
it is I who fashioned myself
for some departed eye.
I can see the pant leg filled
and the shirt stuffed
standing in that crowded room
calling out to play
unthinking
but aware another night is passing.
No, I cannot and will not return.
that skin lies lifeless.
it is gone
and I have a straight face.

Mandate
(For the angry young warrior)

I am sick
and tired
of your mouthing-off
What you say has been said
  (time & time again)
playing out your beer guzzling
prime-time
cowboy fantasy
You who prefer to exit into another world
into some kind of time warp
think of children on a slide
a razor

You educated you
know-it-all
middle of the road
mouthy lovely mystic
Equality and Justice
              and Compassion
(such vague terms!)
have not yet triumphed

There is no Hollywood sunset
and no rider sinking into it
There is no dial to touch
We are here
        Touch this spot
        this Earth
        We share

8 o'clock Monday Morning

Cracked sunlight leaks
through a pane of glass
filling the measured hour.
I slip a red necktie
over my head
and pull it tight
 (as if this
   must be done).
The silky noose
extends from me
like an extra tongue.

Night Vision

Thunderbird wrings out sky
against this tethered apartment
while across the street a woman
walks the rain
strained
through car headlights
                splashing past.

Overhead a crane constructing
a skyscraper shuts down
concrete slabs suspended
      flutter
twigs snap leaves stick
to the window: construction
destruction, a circle
almost complete.

A sliver cracks
daylight fiercely
    swoops
heavily upon the woman
who turns up her collar
in the instant of light, shivering
the known the unknown.

Wet realization upon her
she begins to run
as though chased
as I rise
to pull sound
down tight around me
to block out
the approaching
              ambulance.

Descent

sky
    descends
        behind
            crust moon
spreads raven night.
and you poised on snowshoes
draw in the length
of lake between the pines
as you would
a breath
to notice your presence carved
into the curve of earth.

the constant forest pulses
arranges itself
to life and death. a wolf stalks
darkness. someone
will follow
someone always has
at first getting lost
in the drift
panicking like the hunted
until recognizing
the trail
an ability to return.

The Storm

Sitting behind glass
I can see the sky stir
while over the radio comes a warning
to stay indoors: wind, rain and hail.

A black cloud temporarily blots out the sun.

Somewhere there is more power than I will ever
understand. The ability to create and destroy
in one final sweep. Call it God. Call it Nature.
Call it whatever you Believe. No matter
there it is, there in front of me, emptying the streets.

If I step out of this room and into the storm
Will I feel any closer to this suddenness?
Will I feel like my ancestors?
Will I simply be the modern stranger
confused, wet and alone?

I know that I do not speak the language of thunder
and the radio attempts to persuade me
against making any unnecessary moves.
Yet move I must from deep in the city
out the front door. To get my head soaked and filled
until I am inside the storm.

Voice
(For Leonard Peltier)

When I was corralled
two eagles appeared from a cloud
and lent their path of braille
across the sky.
I felt
followed and was free.
Reaching a clump of pines
I rested. Not knowing my direction
I prayed to the spirits of the earth
and the hereafter: give me strength
                give me strength
                   strength.

The moon was a lamp.
I moved on quickly
away from a life of prison.
A row of fields stretched in line
cultivated clean as a cell.
My people hoped I could fly.
I could not. I was caught.
There is no moon now.
We are what we are
and always shall be.

Passage

I

Dividing time into journey, there is no easy route
they tell. The sky is for you
and against you. The strongest must take the lead,
become shelter, hold course like a sail
bearing the pull and strain of rigging and mast
all for a length of common good.

II

Their lines pleat the sky, a motion transecting
street-line order, the definition of a curb,
redefining the constructs of building,
elevator traffic. With a simplicity
pronounced as warmth to cold, light
to dark, they rise and fly,
taking to a chessboard timetable, each
move instinctively calculated, bright
as sun, moon and star.

III

The geese are trailing spring home to the north end
of the sky. At last, carrying stories
from where the earth neglects winter
and warms sinew and feather. Repetitious geese tales
merely honk to the untuned.

IV

There is no easy route they tell, fearing no evil,
alone together in life and death
joined to both.

Theatre Indigenous

In brief you say they take the land
like common bandits armed with the wrath
of law and greed. Consider it.
Families lined up like trees,
limbs spread and sliced.
You say women and children alike
uprooted drying brittle leaves
on the edge of a newly consecrated road.
And we are wrong, man is forged
in the image of man -- the thirstiest beast.

What you recount are more or less symptoms.

Take this setting:
first a forest silence,
the lighting is dimmed,
a night sky. Move in.
Abruptly the sound from your throat
cries out childlike.
Focus, closer, shift perspective by star
or moonlight and your eyes are stained
with red ochre.
The mascara of ritual complete
you too ooze through village landscape
your blood siphoned from freshly cut wounds
to be planted.

The earth becomes fertile animals grow fat.

Sahquakegick

Although I never knew him
I am told when my great-great-grandfather
signed away miles of home and bush
                        campfires hugged Lake
                        Biscotasing like moons
in treaty, with the government of Canada
                        official men in official
                        black suits
It is a special day he pronounced
looking stern and proud
                        in this photograph
                        shot in front of the Hudson Bay Company
                        store
while faces in the background
looking bewildered looked on

And he knew also the momentous day
meant change
                        change, yes, like the seasons
                        he knew that
and standing like the trunk of a tree
dressed in leather and balancing
his rifle, I am told he said slowly
in grave concern
looking beyond the heads of all
to me now, squarely,
some will learn
and speak.

Poem For Duncan Campbell Scott

(Canadian poet who "had a long and distinguished career
in the Department of Indian Affairs, retiring in 1932."
The Penguin Book of Canadian Verse)

Who is this black coat and tie?
Christian severity etched in the lines
he draws from his mouth. Clearly a noble man
who believes in work and mission. See
how he rises from the red velvet chair,
rises out of the boat with the two Union Jacks
fluttering like birds of prey
and makes his way towards our tents.
This man looks as if he could walk on water
and for our benefit probably would,
if he could.

He says he comes from Ottawa way, Odawa country,
comes to talk treaty and annuity and destiny,
to make the inevitable less painful,
bearing gifts that must be had.
Notice how he speaks aloud and forthright:
      This or Nothing.
      Beware! Without title to the land
        under the Crown you have no legal right
      to be here.
Speaks as though what has been long decided wasn't.
As though he wasn't merely carrying out his duty
to God and King. But sincerely felt.

Some whisper this man lives in a house of many rooms,
has a cook and a maid and even a gardener
to cut his grass and water his flowers.
Some don't care, they don't like the look of him.
They say he asks many questions but
doesn't wait to listen. Asks
much about yesterday, little about today
and acts as if he knows tomorrow.
Others don't like the way he's always busy writing
stuff in the notebook he carries. Him,
he calls it poetry
and says it will make us who are doomed
live forever.

Man To Man

I know there is pain and suffering I have never known
so when they tell me of the old world holocaust
and say no words exist to describe the horrors
I agree
and immediately my mind in searching for an image to understand
flicks to those paintings of damnation the pious ones carried
along with the crucifix and blind faith to the new world.

Christoforo Colombo Claims America, 1492
(Upon the occasion of the Pope's visit to the NWT, 1987)

I

Those who made the journey believed
in God and His goodness. Provider
of hope. Back home many people starved -- but
not all. A King, someone claiming a divine right
to wealth and power, ruled alongside the Church
which in turn claimed God and hope.
(Let's just say that between them they had all
the angles covered.)

II

High noon and drummers chant
under spruce bows. Fancy Dancers whorl
round as I admire blanket patterns in sunlight.
The South American Indian guests
at the microphone translate an ancient Chief:
We're all in this together. Recognize
and renew your strengths.
In shade looking out, I think of understanding
and energy.

III

Both King and Church had much
in common. Both believed Explorers were opportunists.
Necessary. Loyal only if controlled, if rewarded.
Explorers lived a deep fear, endured sky, sea,
the unknown. Lived for gold and plunder
and were Heros when they did. After the fast
came the plenty. And plenty of it.
Titles and Women. Song and Dance
in the streets of Seville.

IV

Once I stared out to the sea from high in a castle
and thought distance and time. Enough
to bring a smile to Carl Jung's lips
as he clasps his hands and says in a deliberate
hushed tone: about your dreams...
Worlds collide. Satellites blast-off
in a flash to send back photographs
while the dancers smile
for the clicking camera.

V

Up at Fort Simpson a conference
will bring together Elders and Youth
announces the Grand-Speaker.
The Pope will visit.
The Prime Minister and
Governor General will greet him.
Drums will beat time to Mother Earth.
Explorers will have come
and gone. America will have been claimed.

Settlers

Tonight you are safe, your
family is safe, behind
the walls you've built,
logs peeled perfectly
hammered into place.
But out there is the bush,
where you feel things lurk
ready to kill and devour.

So each night you lock yourself
in and listen to animal sounds,
watch for the bush to stir.
There are also other sounds
you hear dark and wild, the ones
you think are human
but aren't quite sure.

These sounds you approach only
in the safety of daylight
and never alone
and unarmed.
When we see you coming
we greet you with our best voices
and ask, What is it you fear?

The Man

The man comes towards me.
His hands are bound behind his back.
He asks me to forgive him.
I do not know this man.
I have never seen him before.

He is a face.
A face I can break if I choose.
The man falls to his knees and pleads.
He attempts to kiss my boots.
He almost spoils their shine.

Soon a corporal enters.
He excuses himself and salutes.
He grabs the man by the scruff of the neck.
Again he excuses himself.
The man is hauled away for disciplining.
I do not involve myself in this matter.

At the mirror I pick a speck of lint off my uniform.
I check my profile and admire the brass.
Back at my desk I put up my feet.
I notice where his lips touched the black leather.
This annoys me.
Finally I buzz for the next.

Claim

In sleep the earth reclaims herself
and so I see myself walking
among sparse thin trees,
roots snake-like below my feet
weaving a secure home. Among stone
some determined farmer once piled
in trying to claim what he thought was his,
a cairn to failure, a burdensome reminder.

In my hands this one is smooth,
round and heavy. This stone
of sweat
which these young trees now feed upon.

And further on, another stone but this one a boulder.
I stretch to reach the top, extend my arms
to grasp it, but I am dwarfed in this shadow
of the elemental force that pushed it here
to stand with all the weight of a crucifix.
What did the farmer do?
with both hands already open and raw.

Did he dare even touch it? Or just grunt
and wipe his forehead and try
to work around it. Did he suddenly see his toil slip
between the cracks? Aware that his freshly cleared field
was only waiting for him to die.

The soil here is thin, slabs of rock white
and inexorable scrape the sky as they push for heaven.
He must have seen this
known it like he knew his own aching blood.
How could he not have thought
of leaving? at least once,
of giving the land back.

Or by this time was he himself too full of stone
to leave,
despite knowing with his heavy heart
that if he could not
his son would.

The Other Side Of The Looking Glass
(An Ode to Modern America)

Wash the smog from your eyes, the exhaustion,
the accumulation of years
and examine yourself closely

your teeth are perfect plastic
your hair is someone else's
your skin is pulled and stitched
your face is stretched young
your smile is permanent

Now look closer   Look into the eyes
examine them thoroughly

your family dies or disappears
your friends are enemies
your lovers are sick
your children are strangers
your home is some apartment
your education means nothing
your work even less
your body is a commodity
your wars are big business
your leader is a rich politician
your preacher is god
your god is forsaken
your memory is gone
your luck is finished
your days are numbered
your legacy is a plea
for forgiveness

Creating a Country

They came to North America in search of a new life,
clinging to their few possessions, hungry for prosperity.
They'd had enough poverty and suffering to last a lifetime.
And so they believed with all their hearts
that if they laboured they would all become barons
in a classless society. Patriots were thus born
on both sides of the border. But the process of creating
a country took much longer than most ever imagined.
For there were a myriad of unforeseen obstacles
in this formidable new land. Like mosquitoes and Indians.
Undaunted, the pioneering spirit persisted.

In Canada, Susanna Moodie arrived to take notes.
After writing anti-slavery tracks in England,
she thought it only natural to document the burden
of roughing it in the bush. Susanna shied away
from both mosquitoes and Indians. One day, however,
quite by accident, she met a young Mohawk
whom she thought handsome and for a period flirted
with the notion of what it would be like to be swept away
by him. But she soon tired of such thoughts and nothing ever
became of it. Later she would say neither Indians nor mosquitoes
make good company. She did make it perfectly clear
that she bore no grudge. She believed everything has a place.

Just as she believed her place was across the ocean,
but she too had heard stories of golden opportunities.
Lies! She could be heard screaming. Nothing but lies!
Susanna also believed she was turning life into art
and creating the first semblance of culture
in a godforsaken land.
It was her only compensation.
When she spoke about her life her eyes rolled in her head
like a ship leaving port. She never gave up the dream
of returning home. Dreamed so hard
that even on her death bed she never stopped
talking to herself.

South of the border, Lt. Col. George Armstrong Custer
never once worried about mosquitoes.
It's said that he too was interested in culture
and for this reason carried a gun.

He was a soldier, not an artist, and made no pretence
about it. Custer rarely wrote and never spoke
unless formally addressed. Yet, he was a passionate man
who dreamed the same dream every night.
He fancied that he had discovered the final solution.
Each night he rounded up all the buffalo
in what is now Montana and shot every last one of them.

As a son of European peasantry, he had heard stories
about what it was like to go hungry.
He also knew Indians could starve
just like white people. As a patriot,
he believed his solution was perfectly reasonable.
He also believed American politicians
would see to it that both the buffalo and the Indian
would find a new home
on the American nickel.

Susanna Moodie never met General Golden Hair (as Custer
was affectionately called), she never liked Americans anyway.
She was an old lady of 73 when he died young on the plains
of Little Bighorn trying to live out his dream.
They say that Custer was singing,
"The Girl I Left Behind Me" the day he headed west.
We know he wasn't singing to Susanna Moodie.
We also know that after hearing what the U.S. Cavalry
was doing south of the border, Susanna thought
about the anti-slavery tracks she had written years before
and, for a brief moment, about what had ever become
of her young Mohawk,
if he fared any better.

What Kind of Man

What kind of man
would think of searching for a stick
of exact length and thickness
fasten a nail to the end of it
and jab it again and again
through the head of a turtle
trying to escape into its useless shell
and then after the mess was completed
dump that death into boiling water
so he could peel the shell
away from the flesh
and make it into an ashtray?
This kind of man
we can only try
to understand.

Almighty Voice

One Arrow Reserve 1895
a whiteman's buffalo wanders on dusty land
facts -- the events relate themselves
striving to reach conclusions.

Some say and believe to this day
it was slaughtered to make broth
            a sick child waits
and to others
an almost erotic delight
succumbing to that urge
to defy
the law
(the fences was it the fences?).

Shooting a Northwest Mounted Policeman
death held your hand
            not always a strange companion
while two other companions
chose to walk beside you.

Stillness is now your blanket
like prairie grass
            growing cloudy
in a grandfather's head.

Crow Children

Crows on branches
children
trekking across day
surround them.

Come
to shoot crow.

Waiting on
one anxious moment
Bullet flame
against blackness.

Hunters they.

These children
who kill.
Living a forest
of blood memory.

Let The Oppressed Sing

(For the Native people who fill Canada's prisons
and for all those who continue to struggle for Justice)

Let the oppressed sing of Chile,
the Ojibway who last night
told me he had just got out of prison
after being inside for eight years,
the warrior who lifted his tattooed arm
to the ceiling which for a moment
became the sky
and clenched his fist in proud defiance
looking me straight in the eye
after being told that I too had Ojibway blood.

Let the oppressed sing of Chile,
that Anishanabe who excused himself for drinking,
but said he only wanted to have some fun,
that man with the woman nobody else wanted,
that big man who had just been released from
concrete and steel
to a world that for him is
concrete and steel,
that Mississauga who told me there were only
13 hundred of his people left,
and who like so many others of his kind
had fallen between the fiscal cracks
of a corporate society gone money mad.

Let the oppressed sing of Chile,
where Mother Earth has become infected
by nuclear waste,
where Father Sky has become infected
by industrial waste,
where traditional home lands have been flooded,
clear-cut and mined in the name of progress,
where one half of the world's population starves
while the other half grows fat in both body
and mind,
where law means wealth and power and a strong arm
carrying a big stick,
and where justice is just another word.

Let the oppressed sing of Chile,
Minnie Sutherland, a Native woman struck
by a car New Years morning in Hull, Quebec,
and dragged to the side of the road
by police officers
just doing their duty (To Serve & Protect?)
while witnesses pleaded
an ambulance be called.

Yes. Let Minnie sing of Chile
along with all those other mothers and children
who have died needlessly, senselessly,
unjustly -- Let all of them sing of Chile.
For Chile is more than a country, it is a people
dispossessed   the world over.

You, Your Father, The Indians and Life
(For Chris)

Thailand. The other side of the world.
You go over there to work and don't come back,
ever.
And I am left standing here, left
with your death in my hands,
a telephone receiver.
And I am expected to take it, as if
it happens every day,
as if life is cheap.

Genocide. I read about it. Attend lectures.
You would have been interested, you said
the Indians would come to your father's house
on Manitoulin Island. They respected him
because
he respected them. He is gone and now
so are you.
And I am standing here refusing
to get sentimental. You would laugh.

Ottawa. I go to the fridge for a beer.
It's all I can do.
I want to call someone, but
there is no one. We are all scattered.
Looking from my window I remember
the article about the Indian kids,
alcoholics, age 8.
Life is made cheap. They didn't even get
the front page. The birds will soon be returning,
the snow is beginning to disappear
into the strong earth.

On Lake Titicaca

Between Bolivia and Peru I forget who I am
and the guides continue to keep course. Here
the waves against the boat and the old man
braced against the tiller are important.
I turn and look directly
at him. Not a word parts his lips
and I think of the depth of the lake
the elixir of rhythm   tradition.

We are out past the reed islands
            past the fishermen
            the birds
out among one another inside
a path deep and blue as a prayer.

The old man's companion decked out in bright wool
cap and sweater fiddles with an old oily motor
he somehow keeps going. Like the old man
his Indian life is carved into his face and
defines his presence and like the old man he knows
he is taking me somewhere I have never been
past everything except ourselves
on this water   under this sky.

Tunisia After The Rain

Hiking through the back-reaches
thumbing my passage
over north Africa
I exit the dirt road among thick
gawking trees and silence.
My decision to short cut
bogs down in mud.
I am circled in my attempt to trudge
out of what looks like a world war
battlefield.

It has rained plentiful and I am caught.

From somewhere a child
his hair dark, his body lean
wedged into black rubber boots.
He gestures -- this is his land
and he is my guide
-- I follow.
Arcing from stone to stone
to islands of solid ground
he instructs me to a grassy slope.
Departing his company I offer money
                              so foolish.
He points a finger to his mouth
and we share bread.

Some
(For George Ryga)

When I read the caption announcing your death
I think of the gnarled hands of immigrants
swinging sledge hammers in dollar-a-day cold,
those same hands plowing
stubborn lives. All that steel
cutting the land, carcasses
of buffalo bleached into winter
and brown children huddled
behind wire. Old stories
rising like tobacco smoke. Some laugh.
Some do not.

And I think of myself as I was, wanting
so much to be myself, wandering
half the world. You said,
look where it began for you. Move
ahead by moving back.
North? But we aim to get out.
The train whistles a dream
south and our roots get stretched
across this country. A city chills
our blood (a kind of longing) and we turn
to drink for lost warmth. Some stop.
Some never do.

I also think of you visiting me and
going through my words. Not
one for compliment, idle talk, you
came to offer advice. You said poetry is a gift.
These days the page is an endless winter,
the words sleep soundly and do not fly
when left alone. You said our responsibility
is to speak. To speak for those who cannot.
A child grows with circles in his eyes
and looks for direction. Some find it.
Some do not.

And finally I think of your summerland,
the basket of cherries you gave
me for my journey back. I split the red flesh
with my teeth and sucked in the juice of wind,
rain and sun. We are all going somewhere.
In kindness is guidance. For a moment
I met you and now you have returned to our Mother
the Earth, to God. Do we not spend our lives
returning. Some believe.
Some know.

January City

To the distant sun current
binding fire
swirling
force
I stand and call out
an eye fixed
within an eye
and ask
in common ceremony
stay
and hold me
in the strength
of your gaze

But the black bird
of the wind
a bird
with a breath
a winter
breath
spreads her wings
over me
blows
into my face
and my tongue
is no longer mine
but has become
a naked
little bird

I place my fingers to my mouth
my lips
are a frozen nest
repelled
the teeth of this bird
snap like icicles
I try to call out
but my bird voice
laughs in my face
and caws
in a pitched voice
There is no warmth
for those lost
in january
city

No Questions Asked

Gradually you lose your tongue
and hardly notice.
How can you? It doesn't fall from your mouth
and you don't bite it off
and swallow it (if you did you probably wouldn't be here).
The process is subtle. For the longest time
you even keep thinking it's still attached
and continue to use it to chew or gargle.
Though all the while you are saying less.
Conversations become a burden, a portage of words.

In your blunted mouth they become gnarled
and convoluted, so you accede, resign yourself
to this mute fate. Soon you learn to live without
a tongue. Who needs one anyway, why speak?
You even begin to enjoy your new position
and use it to your advantage. Your work
and play become a silent and private deal,
while everywhere, in the sky, on the ground,
there are raw signs demanding your voice
and you are empty.
Nothing to say.
No excuses required.
No questions asked.

Sociable

In this bar we drink to get drunk.
Being sociable has nothing to do
with it. We don't even like each other.
So we sit and talk friendship,
blow smoke into each other's face,
butt our cigarettes
in each other's eyes.

For us this is a normal evening.
We've got nothing to lose.
Besides the liquor tastes good
it's like when you bite
your lip and can't stop
sucking your own blood.
No matter how bitter
you begin to enjoy it.

On The Street

he falls face first
pavement springs an embrace
evening collides with buildings
and sky slams
inside her head with a thud
he laughs

him he doesn't feel
for him everything is goddamn
silly laughter which fills her
as she bends
tries to help
hopeless
dead drunk hopeless
weight

she wants to curse
this husband
pedestrians stop
gawk
join his laughter
her tears spilling over him
like a slit wrist

Shine

Into the business of a bar enters
a crippled man
who leans into a clatter
of voices and bottles,
props himself at a table.

Shine's the name,
lost ma leg passed out one night
cross the railroad tracks
big train came 'long
didn't feel a thing.

Buy me a beer and I'll eat this here razor
blade, he says to the unsuspecting crowd
as he takes something shiny
from his shirt pocket,
carefully unwraps it
and slips it into his mouth.

OK, some sport shouts.
Chewing blood begins to dribble
from the corner of Shine's lips
down his chin
as you hear him mumble,
Don't feel a thing.

Untitled

and
I
dreamt
we were
safe
and
warm
in
a land
where all the creature
of earth and sky
spoke freely
and
understood

X X X

AM - Manslaughter   262 06-02

WILLIAMS LAKE, B.C. (CP) - A 16-year old Anaham reserve girl charged with murder was found guilty Tuesday of a reduced charge of manslaughter Tuesday by county court judge.<
   The juvenile girl was charged with murder in the Nov. 16 stabbing death of Sandra Johnny, 16.<
   Police told court the stabbing occurred in the bedroom of a friend's home on the reserve west of this Cariboo community where the two girls had been attending an all-night drinking party.<
   Judge C.C. Barnett said in rendering his decision that the girl, whose name was withheld because of her age, probably couldn't remember the incident and was therefore guilty of the lesser charge.<
   The girl will be sentenced Feb. 11.<

0052es 06-02<

Public Education

I live in a free country where I can get what I want:
education
  profession
    spouse
      house
drive a car, eat in restaurants, in a free country
where prisons hold criminals, courts prove guilt
and there are no bars to upward mobility.

I live in a free country and was glad to look white.
Never said a word when I was taught someone else's history.
In a country where no one had to say there were more
Indians in jail than in school. All I had to do
was look around me.

Pale Face

When I was small
one day I came home crying
because the kids at school
had called my mother Squaw.
I told her what they said
and she said well we are
Indian. I then went directly
to the mirror. After that
I went back to school
to face them.

All these years later I'm told
of a young Cree girl who painted
her face with javex bleach
so she could look pale
like me. Sitting here I wish
I could have been there
to tell her
it would do
no good
and that she was beautiful.

Hospital Visit

Bringing apples, plums and pears for someone else
I pass grey heads in white rooms
scanning the corridor for a sign of recognition.
The disinfected hospital enters the mind
through the nostrils.
We greet.
There was a time when his fingers
were like tree roots -- shake firmly
keep a firm grip, man to man.
Our eyes meet picking up the slack that age
accumulates like loose skin.

Between us there is much to add and subtract.
Precision cannot be shucked casually
like a shrug or a glance.
It is demanded by the creases in our face, in our life.
Like beadwork our stories are suspended
and must be gathered with care.
What is evident is that soon your body breaks,
a cramp in the neck, in the back and that
is just the beginning. Oh, of course there is always
the temporary relief -- firm massaging hands
naked thighs -- but it never lasts long enough.

Story: There are two young men hunched and drumming.
A ritual of feathers in their hair.
There is no other sound. The beat is hard
and steady and lasts long into the night.
Come the black and white of morning
the fire between them is transparent. No longer
are there sparks shooting their animal eye sharpness.
Only the outline of the drummers remain.
They become something else:
another life
another story.

Again I see you in a forest among the pines.
The setting seems to change little, if at all.
This time perhaps it is winter, a northern winter,
dogs howling, wind and snow cold.

On the trapline or delivering the Queen's mail
strength is your ally. Endurance keeps you
going and some kind of dedication, to exactly what
I am uncertain. Straining
through moments of silence you find difficulty
in expressing yourself.
Sitting next to the bed, wrapped in a blanket,
you say they suggested you change
your name, give up your identity.
So you did (or so everyone thought).
They said that you could probably make it
in the system.
So what if you couldn't read or write.
You would succeed
at all costs.

Perched fourteen floors up you wait
as if in a swaying watchtower. For you
traffic smudges are fires on a forest horizon,
soot a hot exhaust. Will your bush sense, your sixth
sense, somehow get you through?
You are the crew-boss. Your name is called.
The clouds are setting in like a prayer.
You say be thankful they hold rain. Your crew
laughs while you remain quiet
thinking about your work and the vague notion
of equality among men.
There is no time for idleness
you grab a shovel.

What does it mean to you, I wonder,
to lie between cold hospital sheets
for the first and last time and know it.
The trail, a life once stripped of the non-essentials
buried somewhere deep inside you.
I wonder if there will be a flood
in the operating room? I mean
after the surgeons make the first incision.
Will they be suddenly plunging their hands
into icy river water?
Will there be a snow storm?
Tell me.

Admittance: Visiting hours 2:00 - 9:00.
A nurse stands in the doorway.
I will not tell her
of a memory filled with rivers and lakes.
I cannot explain the calluses worn into your hands
or the stoop of your shoulders. Halfway through the knot
of a portage the blackflies descend. The cut
of the tumpline across the forehead.
One thing is for certain: I cannot remain.
Forests cover footprints; the city covers me.

Proclamation: From now on let us hold to the ways
of the young and the wise.
Let us savour the smoke,
and drink hard for the last time,
dance beside the railroad tracks,
toss knives and then swim in clean water.
We will speak
of our dreams and share everything
we always wanted.
We will laugh like children eating fruit.

December

Here you walk the wet city,
streets turned to crevices,
blinding light from the 24 hour gas station
shining like a tumour,
head filled with news of knifings,
a 12 inch army surplus blade
                       with mandatory dinosaur edge.
Cannot help but think it all so
grim.

The last thing you want to do is complain,
point a finger (at who?) but you are waiting on bended
no broken
knee
for someone to explain   at least hint
why?

Three muggings yesterday
a man walking home, a woman
putting out the trash,
an elder punched,
her purse snatched.

At a time like this it is hard to think love,
the pattern of a look
intricate as a leaf,
blouse and brassiere over a wooden chair,
moon rippling on window sill
glancing up
         to her naked shoulders.

Faces stare, memory dries
and plugs your pen.

And still you remember christmas eve
driving home through deep bush
fresh snow high as trees,
the car careening out of control
from bank to bank, spinning
to a standstill on the edge of a bridge.

And later standing over the rushing water,
arms around each other,
                              embracing life
more than ever before.

On this note
mail her the bluish kiss
of a wild orchid and hope
and pray that all affidavits filed in a drop of tear
shall be withdrawn.
There is still time
to open doors with the blessed invitation
of poetry, lips fluid
as an Ojibway waterdrum,
arms the stones that bind and tune.
A knife cannot slice love.

Conversation

That was in Ottawa, on laurier street
before they tore down the old brick buildings
and put up highrises that swallowed the afternoon sun.
You buzzed my room
not for love but for rest,
to sleep on the sofa.
    I threw a blanket over you,
and in the morning you kissed me shyly
and we talked
    and laughed over breakfast.
Then you were gone
   (back to your man,
    one of them)
and I lost sight of you,
just as I lost my voice over you
writing at the kitchen table,

   I know our conversation
   will not last
   the birds are seeking spring
   innocent traitors
   unhesitantly winging their sky
   slight and lost
   as blossoms or tufts of willow
   leaving us down on snow:
   a delicate sadness.
   And I am thinking of your lips
   and the words that will make
   a memory soft and warm
   curling like clouds
   from our morning coffee.

Now, almost as an aside, he tells me you're dead,
just like that,
a bad heart? a broken vessel in the brain?
    he's not sure,
a broken heart? a rupture of memory?
    neither am I.

But then it happened years ago,
and this is another city,
another time
of wives and children,
and we are simply on our way to buy wine
for the barbecue.
There isn't much we say   except
agree on the delicate kind of person
you were,
consider your absence,
your flight.

Demand

She digs me up
in her letter
turns grey earth
black, spreads freshness
and out sprouts hardened memory: face, hair, hands, breasts, thighs,
eyes, laughter and tears, popcorn and whisky,
even a room and a street, a clang of streetcars,
a whole damn city.
       from now on I will accept only
       phone calls
       this kind of inky cultivation
       she directs
       is too permanent
       and unbelievable
       for me
        here.

Trickster

He is on a balcony beside a moon
blooming spring
and stiff-legged birds.
She is below beside trees
oblivious
to his feathered shadow.

He watches this woman
momentarily fixed to insects
beating streetlight
her abrupt high heels
clicking pavement
as she tightens her scarf
like a silk rope, a wish
for arrival.

He watches and becomes
a part of her, a sound
hovering inside.
When she finally looks up
she smiles and waves
at his perched presence
when she sees him
as he might be.

He calls her to join him.
She doesn't understand
his kind of old language
doesn't know
he has been expecting her
all these years.
She has been expecting him.

Emotion

I wake after dreaming of hummingbird,
holding myself perfectly still
over your body. Opening my eyes
I look around the white room
to make sure I know where I am.

Strange that you still tried to speak
about him, even as I hovered in the air
beating my wings furiously,
feeding on your sweetness.
Your arm outstretched, you pointed north
to a painting you were having difficulty completing.

You called it emotion
and brought me to a confusion of colour,
a rainbow poured over a glass of ice.
You said there had been another woman.
And that you had wanted
to get pregnant.

Poetry

makes me
want to write poetry,
exotic disease I guess,
      butterfly palpitations
bursting across the kitchen table
fragrance of sweetgrass
and wild mint wafting into the room,
      jasmine tea
      for two
suddenly on the boil,
      whistling intimacy,
warming what is inside,
perfection of nipple, im-
perfection of heart,
arc of arm,
shape of (tender?) greeting,
(bitter?) farewell,
extended from toe to thigh to infinity.

nothing to do with
I can do better
nothing like that, this honest desire
that kicks
like a new born calf
jumping up and disappearing
into its own geography.

Chant For Mother and Child

                        prairie grass flows

I will be a sparrow
perched on your body
softness slowly rustling

                        prairie grass flows

I will be a wind
washing past
cooling you gently
and in the morning

                        prairie grass flows

I will be a dew
cleansing
a rainbow arc
revealing
the many colours of our day

                        prairie grass flows

Influences

one window too high to reach,
a room in darkness,
husbands beating wives the colour of night,
swollen eyes
seeing what some refuse to admit
  (You, have you been there?)
and children   running
through that darkness
                children
who have no idea
where they are going,
when they are too small to even make it
over the fence, the locked gate,
these children
jumping from moving cars
or cars momentarily stopped
                at liquor stores or bars,
children depending on their dogs
for protection and love.

a small town explodes
in a night of alcohol fists
        turning brain
into anguish and hate,
snow and distance piling in on itself
isolating and smothering.
  (And like you, no one tells.)

television boredom, broken furniture,
wrecked cars, bottles
        filled with tears
and stacked in the bedroom,
traded in for deposit,
all the while our elected members of Parliament
merrily singing
"life is just a bowl of cherries,"
singing and arguing for first place,
for expense cheques
                and suburban comfort,

politicians who gave up believing
in small towns,
politicians who never did believe,
who never stood under one black window
too high to reach
and whose children never will.

Hunter

When we dragged his body
by rope and hook from the bottom
of the lake and threw our quick eyes into his
there was nothing: no pain, no remorse
                          anger or despair.
Bloated and veined, inside out for all to see,
like someone who should have known better,
Was this the same man who had hunted the local scene
(with knuckles red and ready,
                                penis like a flag or a weapon)
ready for a drunk, a fight, a fuck, a combination
plate of entertainment?

Something gripped and pulled him
from his wife and child, strung him along
through loin and up out of mind and matter,
clung with a weight heavier
than even his corpse.

Surely Not Warriors

black leather
and pink porcupine hair
believing birth and history are against them
on the corner bumming spare change
waiting on party-time.
is this rebellion
    or resignation?
only their hairdressers know for sure.

10 Park Poems

1

In this park old men see themselves
in the wet, staggered on benches,
crumpled in polyester. They
recognize their sounds
for what they are
grunting a prolonged
existence.

2

In this park old men see themselves cursed
too afraid to die
too afraid to live
while others just see
themselves sick
and tired.

3

In this park old men see
they are past asking for quarters
and take what they have
and drink it
until their wet heads suck air
and they dive onto the street
for more.

4

In this park old men see
what they have to see.
Most times they forget
they ever had a family
their minds long dredged
of that life. They forget
to nobody's surprise
not even their own.

5

In this park old men see through mucous eyes.
Some almost too ashamed to ask for handouts
their twisted limbs shaking.
Here there are flowers
and trees and even fountains.
Children yelp and play tag
while mothers
push strollers.

6

In this park these men see few happy scenes
but then these men slobber,
leave happiness
to the new.

7

In this park you can see an old man
called grandfather. Call him wanted.
Maybe tomorrow someone will strap him to a bed
and try to turn back the clock.
Sober him up so that he can start over.
In this park there are those
who want to help
but cannot.

8

In this park you can see the dead walk.
The crippled. The
defeated. Those who gave
up on tomorrow
stumbled one way.

9

In this park you can see old men
who want out
sometimes.

10

In this park you can also see youth
broken, veins tied black
as dirty oceans
eyes sunk.

Long Distance

A church tolls the sabbath, guides
the passersby, and I find myself
thinking of those European women who wear black
for the rest of their lives.
Today life unwinds itself and leaves me
standing in loss. Family
has died.

But this bell is not for her.

It is for those on the street below
who weep,
drink sherry or whisky, clutch
a bible, a rosary, an obituary,
a plot in a cemetery. A memory
that once could breathe, laugh, cry,
smell flowers,
say hello, goodbye,
or even daughter, son.

I am unfamiliar miles, a stream

of steady years coursing through me
like a great eagle flapping a lengthening shadow,
and I am charged in the power
day conjures
to inform me
of the distances I live.

Old Story

The story she tells spirals out a time before
your birth, before even hers.
An old story that sounds new, that rises
like the steam from both your cups,
yet has nothing to do with cracked cups,
unmatched plates, half bottles of rye,
National Enquirer in the outhouse,
flies sneaking in through holes in the screen,
lumber picked up along the roadside and
banged together, beer bottles,
and ashtrays full of butts.

Nothing to do with that, the thing
that rises like night, like water
from deep in remembered earth
out of forgotten memory.
The thing that sounds like coming rain
and makes eyes blink round when wind creaks
through houses and old timber tells
of an older life, a path bordered by jackpine
and birch leading down to Misshipeshu of the lake,
emerald eyes and skin of gold scales, a path
to red snake, black pike and family.

Come. Under this star blanket, splinter of moon,
her voice guides your footsteps along islands
of solid earth. Where are you going?
She says to the dream where else. To the part
that must be found out, where one day
you can return on your own.
(Does she actually say this
or are you now just dreaming?)
And almost as soon as she begins you are back
at the kitchen table, your hand
gripped to a cold cup of tea, the clock
hitting supper time.

With These Hands

with these hands, these long
lithe hands I was born with
take with me
that strapped on snowshoes
so my feet could walk
towards
a half-remembered lake
winters away
knowing where it was
but no longer what
it was

these same hands
that fumbled with frozen fishing line
when there was nothing
to hold
but a piece of ice
& sky
with these hands
I cupped & placed
to my mouth
& blew into
I trumpet
survival

Home

I

No, there is no regretting it
I am not home.
Like most I took my first step
and continued,
adapted (to my surprise thinking about it)
as if slow-gaited, rheumatic, congested,
a child who matures in midwinter,
someone who remembers stiff clothes thawing
limbs leaking over a fire,
frozen eyelids, nightly storms and icicles
sprouting strange plants.

II

Inside a cool cafe the woman explains
that she has travelled the world,
has lived in numerous countries
and no matter where she goes
she always brings her Canadian room,
transports her colonial pine furniture,
even drinks "Canadian Club" on special occasions,
buys Canadian books
and stays abreast of the news
all for a glimpse of home.

III

Me, I am not home
I suppose mine is still back there,
where the wind still whistles
like some weary bird
who cannot or will not ever leave,
in a land where trees are split in preparation
for the next drop of the thermometer,
where alcohol washes down almost everything,
where books belong somewhere else
and there is no news.

Their Own

In this country famous for banks
and efficiency
where time is jewellery
worn with pride
we find ourselves strolling
with no direction
caught
beside rush hour's
blank-eyed scream.

Our own eyes fixed
on office towers lit
by waves of sun, glass
candles
which make us wonder
aloud
who or what
is burning inside.

At the store "Aquatic Life"
three tanks move
deep in the window
and so we stop and watch
the strange suck
and expel of light
the bug-eyed antennas
the flat lips and blue
whiskers -- the mystery
so near.

We are about to leave
when a tail flashes
and draws us
to the furthest tank
where a swarm is fiercely occupied.
Our faces pressed to the glass
we manage to see
through the bubbled stir
how they tear at the flesh
of one of their own
weakened
but not yet dead.

Once We Went Fishing

Remember waking the sun
packing Dad's old canvas sack
and starting for the trestle, eating
our lunch before we even got halfway there.
Oil along the tracks soaking up
so much heat we thought our runners
would melt and stick to our feet.

Finally relief in the shade.
We perched ourselves on the cement ledge
baiting hooks, dangling our feet
in the cool current, while
trains above periodically roared
and made me think of the city.

Today I ate the fish you caught
yesterday. Naturally they were delicious.
When you gave them to me
I packed them in ice and drove south
all night and into the next day.
Let me begin by thanking the fish.

Protect The Island

Across the midsummer sun
an aluminum boat.
Suddenly aware.
I watch it approach
measure distance
in the blink of an eye.

Lifted from a solitude of loons.
I stand.
Protect the island.
It's a lifesaver.
You can't take it with you.
It's a breath of fresh air.

Six vacationers land,
slurring themselves.
Whisky walk.
I approach. My lungs full and tense.
They call: Where are the fish?
I reply: In the north channel, but they're belly-up.
The rain is vinegar.

Cursing
they say they will write Washington
and Ottawa
and it won't be love letters.
They salute
pile into the boat and shove off.
At the shore trees bow
in the recent wind
offering the greatest applause.

The Trout Become The Day Later That Evening
(For Tony)

the warm december afternoon embankment
off the roadside, the slippery snow beneath our feet,
the slide down to the lake, the
minnow pail in my hand,
the steel auger in yours, the packsacks
jammed full

the lines we set to make the catch,
the white sun on the ice we
stand on and drill through,
even the willows we grab to keep balance
to stop ourselves from sliding back down
on our way back up

everything: it all fills our plate, swims
into us

Kebsquasheshing

The Kebsquasheshing floats through my back door,
carrying my youth, the fishing rod I dropped overboard
fifteen years ago, carrying the pike and their pike dreams
of barbless lures, fat worms and clean water.

Today I tear into <u>The Globe and Mail</u> searching
for an article explaining why the transformer blew
spewing hundreds of gallons of PCBs
into the water. Discover there is no explanation.

Ontario Hydro blameless. No harm done.
And still we drink and the water continues
past us, past the newspaper, up and out to the Arctic.
Where big fish eat small fish and dream clean.

Poem For Esher (In memory)

The northern bush gives him his livelihood
he has spent all his years there -- maybe 60
and with sons and neighbours
and familiar-faced dogs
has guided Americans
to the heart of the kill
whether with high-powered rifle
or bow and arrow
photo-albums show grinning faces
and black bear-head trophies

The bush is life
it is a mutual affair
sunrise and sunset
merging over the years
from yesterday's yellow half-ton
with the burnt-out clutch, to
today's muscle truck

And now at times he must pause
knowing his way can never last
his circuit, arteries, veins,
the bush roads,
have been worn thin
like the barrel
of another stranger's gun

After the Hunt

Shall we parade his head
lashed to a truck? Refuse
to accept spirit flight, narrow
vision, block last light?
Or shall we let him rise like a great
silent bird to catch the attention of a mother
and her sons?

Today I slip on my moccasins
hide fraying
soles worn
beaded flowers shedding petals
And I think of my brother slitting
the moose's thick throat
while I take hold
hot blood over both my hands.

And between the pines our mother
begins to make her way
towards us, as we
once made our way out of her
hush of bush telling
our presence, telling everything
there is to know.

Rock Bottom Lake

a pictograph painted on the east face
of an overhanging cliff alive
with moss, you see it as direction,
as belonging, a gift
not to be refused.

alone and cool, night
and curtains move
as if by will,
easily from an open window.

what sound there is comes from you.

inside -- outside, no longer
is there even a room,
perhaps the curtains,
a window frame
   suspended
by the weight of itself,
the ability of the moment,
a circling moon.

from bottom through dark
eyes flush to surface
and you rise
like a trout feeding
on this faded detail
this language to be understood.

these strokes are stories
culled from the deepest part
of a people
and you have returned.

The Season
(For Linda)

In a week or so
we will be travelling
these days
it is the season
and it feels good
to be on the move
because before we know it
we've returned
and settled into a stationary existence
of boardrooms and timetables
where we'll find ourselves
pretending
we never had
a loon
        a deer or even a whale
locked inside us
        and wanting out

About the writer:

Armand Garnet Ruffo was born in Chapleau, Northern Ontario, and draws on his Ojibway heritage for his work. His education includes degrees from York University, the University of Ottawa and the University of Windsor; in addition, he has travelled widely and has worked as a harvester of wildrice, a writer-researcher for the (now defunct) *Native Perspective* magazine, an editor with The Native Council of Canada, an officer with the Department of External Affairs, and an Instructor at the En'owkin Centre, an Aboriginal educational institution.

His poetry and fiction continues to be published in literary magazines and anthologies both in Canada and abroad. He was also an invited participant at the *"Returning the Gift"* native writers conference hosted by the University of Oklahoma in 1992.

He currently divides his time between Northern Ontario, Ottawa and Penticton, B.C. This is his first book.

About the artist:

Leo Yerxa was born on the Little Eagle (Ojibway) Reserve near Fort Frances in Northern Ontario, where he lived close to the land, hunting and fishing with his father. Since beginning his artistic career, he has worked in a variety of media and for many institutions, including the Royal Ontario Museum, the Canadian Museum of Civilization and the Royal Canadian Mint.

He is also the author and illustrator of the recent children's book *Last Leaf First Snowflake to Fall*. He now lives in Ottawa, where he continues to work as an artist.